Hope for Neighbors™

For every person we touch,
we leave a small handprint on their heart.
Let that touch be one of hope…

Psalm 118:24 This is the day which the LORD hath made;
we will rejoice and be glad in it.

To

_____

From

_____

Date

_____

Message

_____

_____

_____

Hope for Neighbors™ Wandering through Life

Text Copyright ©2014 by Wendy Nelson
Artwork and Photography Copyright ©2014 by Wendy Nelson

Text Copyright ©2014 by Tamera Striegel
Photography Copyright ©2014 by Tamera Striegel

Published by MediaTek Grafx
POB 62, Bonnieville, Kentucky, 42713

ISBN 978-0-692-30348-1

Design and production by MediaTek Grafx, Bonnieville, Kentucky.

The Publisher has made every effort to avoid errors or omissions. Opinions, articles, stories, recipes and old-fashioned cures are intended for entertainment, motivation for research and future study. This book includes content that is fiction and non-fiction.

Printed in the United States of America

Table of Contents

www.HopeforNeighbors.com

Love Thy Neighbor

Matthew 22:37 Jesus said unto him, Thou shalt love the Lord thy God with all thy heart, and with all thy soul, and with all thy mind.
Matthew 22:38 This is the first and great commandment.
Matthew 22:39 And the second is like unto it, Thou shalt love thy neighbour as thyself.

Fruitfulness in Christ

North Dakota winters can be likened to a never-ending song; one that isn't particularly a favorite tune that lingers in your head. When that season has worn out its extended welcome, spring, summer and fall are cherished and savored immensely; as much as the peak fruits and produce that find their way from local gardens and farmer's markets to our family tables. Juicy pears, brilliantly red cherries marking that mid-season point of the summer; fresh green beans and cucumbers to wash, cut and mix for garden salads - are all waiting to share a plate with grilled burgers, chicken and steak. The neighborhood smells in the air have that distinctive blend of budding trees and flowers, family barbecues and late-night bonfires - all beckoning people to linger outdoors. The bikes come out, the long walks begin; sidewalks and streets fill with people, pets and conversation.

One particular late August day, a long walk with a neighbor turned into an interesting discussion. Topics of weather, jobs, kids, prices of groceries and our own backyard gardens made their way into the conversation. It seemed a particular rough-around-the-edges neighbor in our cul-de-sac might be fond of helping himself to beautiful, plump tomatoes from my friend Carol's huge garden. She never actually saw Tom take any tomatoes, but daily took stock of what she had and was convinced he was taking a few, every so often. They'd had quibbles over trees and property line issues prior to the tomato incidents, so there was dissension already evident in their relationship. This was, I felt, a wonderful

Zechariah 8:16 These are the things that ye shall do; Speak ye every man the truth to his neighbour; execute the judgment of truth and peace in your gates:
Zechariah 8:17 And let none of you imagine evil in your hearts against his neighbour; and love no false oath: for all these are things that I hate, saith the LORD.

opportunity to offer the plausible solution of *turning the other cheek* and suggested just offering him some tomatoes and as a result, he wouldn't have to feel guilty about stealing them (if he was) and she could demonstrate neighborly character in giving him some tomatoes.

She felt a different approach would be more appropriate than what I suggested, and, instead of heeding my advice, proceeded to have her two children deliver fresh cucumbers, tomatoes, and other bounty from their garden, sharing with me and with others in the cul-de-sac, yet skipping his house to share the garden vegetables. I don't know if he was aware of being passed by, but my concern was for the lesson learned by the impressionable children delivering the produce. They were good, giving kids, but I'm not sure if it was truly being 'neighborly' to bypass a certain home in this instance. We cannot judge, none of us are without sin, but it left me feeling kind of empty and bad for the person's place that wasn't a part of their route. Weeks passed, the season gave way to brisker winds, changing leaves, and apples hung heavy from various trees in our neighboring yards. Early one fall evening, Tom showed up at our doorstep. My college-age daughter was standing on the second-floor landing at top of the steps, having the opportunity to listen to Tom's words, when I opened the door. He held a big grocery bag of crisp, cold, just-picked apples from his tree. "I remembered you said that your apple tree you had for years had been knocked down by a storm this last summer, so I thought you could use these," he said

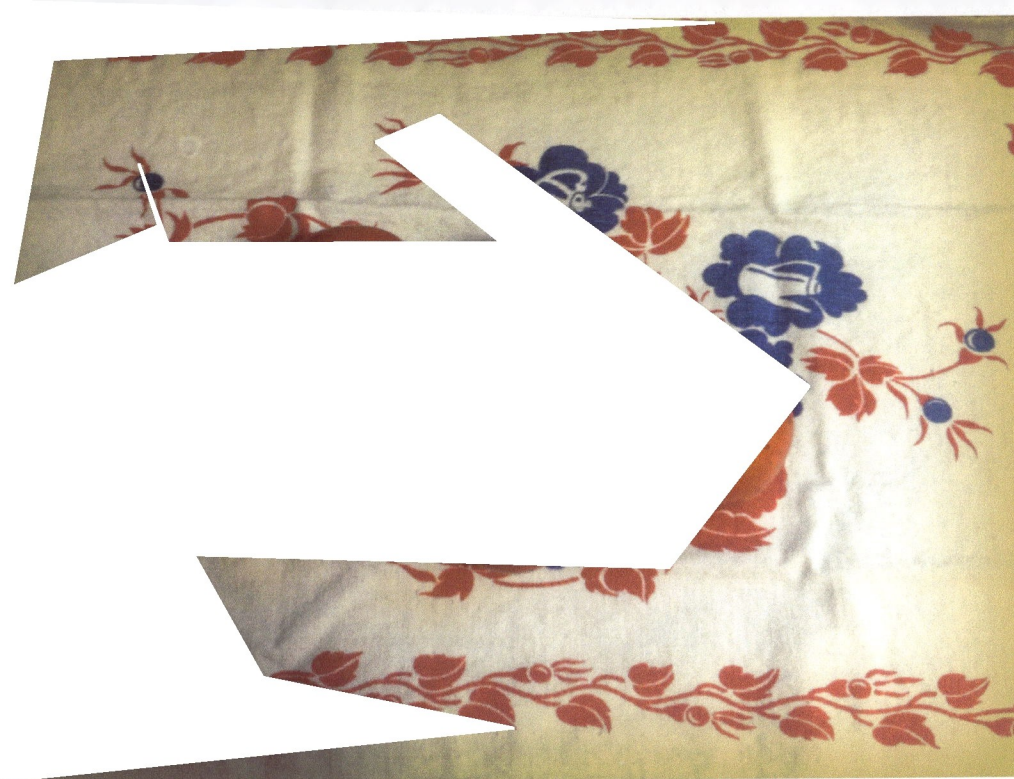

with a sideways grin. Pleasantly surprised, I thanked him, looked up at my daughter after he had left, and she said, "I guess there's some good in all of us, isn't there?" She witnessed a simple act that had lasting meaning. Did I share my story with my neighbor that didn't get along with him? Yes, I did. Did anything change in their relationship? Not at the time, but hopefully there was a seed planted. Do we treat our neighbors the way we tend our gardens? Do we nurture and do we nourish them daily? Are we servants in our response to others? Even if others have sinned, we always have to look at ourselves and our actions. We have to love the sinner and hate the sin.

Jeremiah 31:34 And they shall teach no more every man his neighbour, and every man his brother, saying, Know the LORD: for they shall all know me, from the least of them unto the greatest of them, saith the LORD: for I will forgive their iniquity, and I will remember their sin no more.

Ephesians 3:17-19 That Christ may dwell in your hearts by faith; that ye, being rooted and grounded in love, May be able to comprehend with all saints what is the breadth, and length, and depth, and height; And to know the love of Christ, which passeth knowledge, that ye might be filled with all the fulness of God.

Love thy neighbor...

Titus 2:13 Looking for that blessed hope,
and the glorious appearing of the great God and our Saviour Jesus Christ;
Titus 2:14 Who gave himself for us, that he might redeem us from all iniquity, and purify
unto himself a peculiar people, zealous of good works.

Hope

Hope - what a beautiful, encouraging word in the English language! The word itself suggests something good, beneficial, tangible - something each and every one of us longs for in our daily lives. The dictionary definition of hope is to wish for something with expectation of its fulfillment, to have confidence and trust; to look forward to.

We see hope in the good news of a doctor's diagnosis or viable options for treatment.

We see hope in a person's smile when a friend or relative shares positive news, or talks about how they'll plan a special day together.

We see hope in someone recovering from a serious injury, and in small strides happening daily to gain independence.

We see hope in attaining a job promotion, celebrating birthdays and positive events in our lives that we look forward to with hope, anticipation and promise of better tomorrows.

The Biblical definition of hope gives the assurance of God beside us daily, guiding us, seeing with His eyes a path; a direction for our lives here on earth and our future with Him in heaven. He does not promise a life void of pain or suffering, but He clearly promises He will be with us in the challenges and in the joys of our lives as a foundation - an anchor - for our very being.

"Which hope we have as an anchor of the soul, both sure and stedfast, and which entereth into that within the veil; Whither the forerunner is for us entered, even Jesus, made an high priest for ever after the order of Melchisedec." - Hebrews 6:19-20

What a comfort in the solid strength we feel from His word and His promise - and hope for our existence as one of His children. In our prayers and seeking the knowledge of God, He will give us the ultimate hope for living - living IN Him and FOR Him.

"By whom also we have access by faith into this grace wherein we stand, and rejoice in hope of the glory of God."
- Romans 5:2

bird songs

Sweet summer is alive with the flurry of bird activity. Relaxing by the lake, we feed the birds and it is an awesome experience! Patiently holding out our arms with a small bit of food placed flatly on our open palms, we wait. Finally, if only momentarily, we feel that small flutter and dance of tiny feet as they gather their treats! Our arms might increasingly ache, but we persist, longing for that splendid, fleeting connection that fills us with awe!

Many little calls, warbles and songs can be heard in every season. It is with great anticipation that we search out our little feathered friends. Chatter, song and alerts fill the air. They share their songs with us. We, in turn, feed our little neighbors - to help them through the harsh winters.

Read the Bible and study the Word of God. God gives us hope!

There is a road that leads home.

But, there is a distant fog that seems to hide it from us.
We feel it clearly, see it vaguely and it calls to us
from time to time. For a moment, we dream
of something special we must do
and then it slips away.

dreams

We wander through our days, trying to do our best.
We have this stress that never seems to go away and
we long for a new direction. If we could only see our
Father in Heaven's purpose for our life, we could fulfill
our dreams He has for us.

1 Corinthians 15:58 Therefore, my beloved brethren, be ye stedfast,
unmoveable, always abounding in the work of the Lord,
forasmuch as ye know that your labour is not in vain in the Lord.

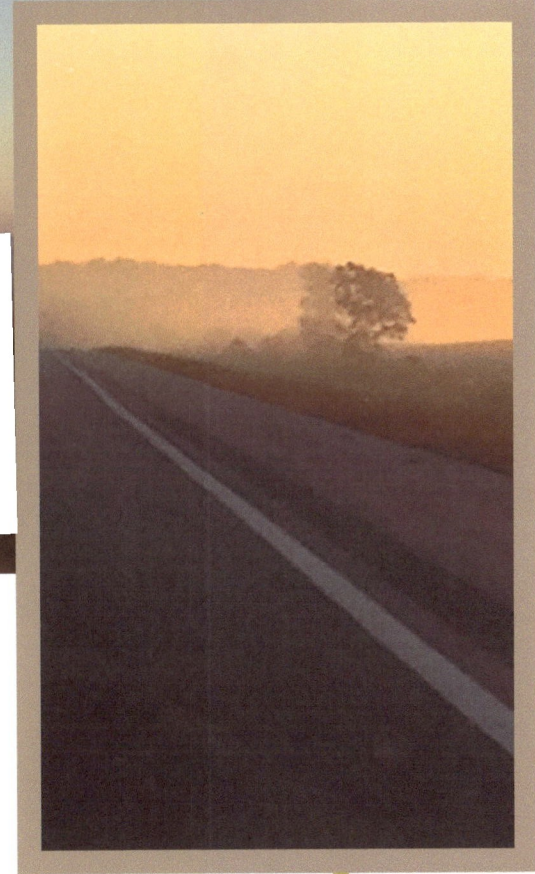

Opportunities to Simplify
A Reflection on Life's Goodness...

Life is very complex, fast-paced, costs so much and is so stressful. Everything is very complicated, happens so fast, is expensive and causes anxiety. That may be the case for some people, but I have taken every opportunity to "simplify" life!

Life does not have to be complex. I slept good last night. I ate my breakfast of Corn Flakes® and coffee. I prayed to God and read His Word. I chose something comfortable to wear and I drove to work. I enjoyed my duties, ate my lunch and visited with co-workers. They talked about life's burdens and I shared how God makes my life easier when I ask Him for help. They asked if that works and I said yes; gave them examples. They seemed a little surprised by this. Later, I had some orange juice and raisins for a snack. A co-worker told me I could get overtime if I worked on Saturday. I told him no; that the weekend time was for my family. I finished my job and started to drive home. On my way home, I reflected on the past and all the crazy things I used to do. Those things kept me away from my family and distracted me from my Father in Heaven. Now, life had changed. I bought a bag of apples from our neighbor, a mile from our home, and shared some laughs with him for a few minutes. I arrived at

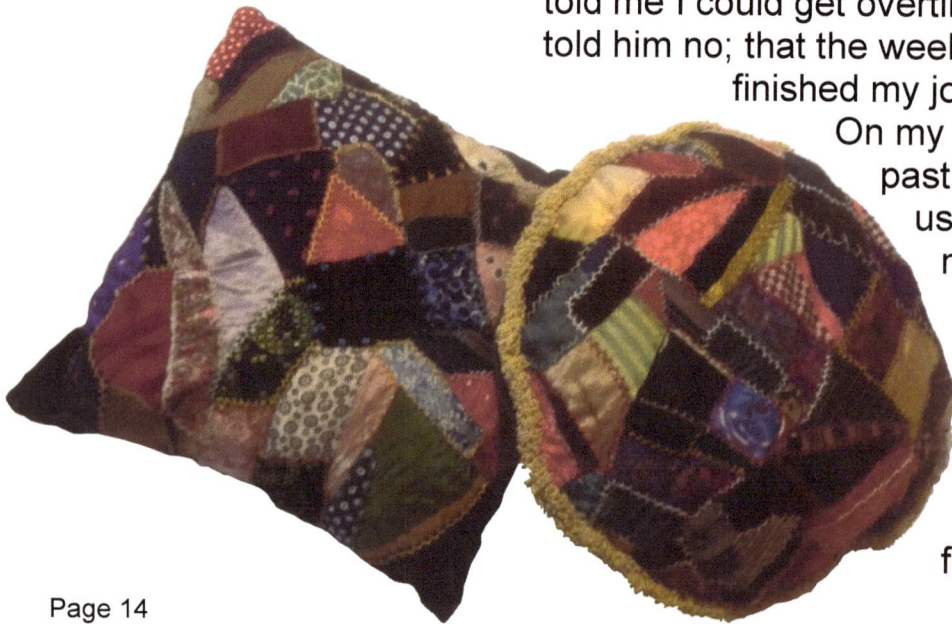

Matthew 6:24 No man can serve two masters: for either he will hate the one, and love the other; or else he will hold to the one, and despise the other. Ye cannot serve God and mammon.

home a little tired, but happy. My family and I laughed and joked around at dinner time. We had a food fight with peas! What a mess, but we had a hilarious time! After dinner we each had an apple, and I played with the dogs. Later, I went for a walk. God makes life simpler for us. Simplifying gives us hope.

Matthew 11:30 For my yoke is easy, and my burden is light.

Life does not have to be fast-paced. I went for a walk at the end of the day and I watched the sun as it was setting. I never realized how many colors there were and I never realized how fast it happens - before all turns black. I like the slower pace that I have chosen to live. We live in the world, but we don't have to be a part of it. I had a few things that seemed like crises today. A couple of them I dealt with in a calm manner; a couple I did not deal with at all. They will probably go away on their own. One item, I will deal with in a day or two, after I pray about it. Also, one of my friends said there was a great deal on something I could buy, but I had to act today or I would miss out. I said, "Okay." I was okay with missing out. No decision made quickly is a good one. I used to do things fast and I missed out on a lot that I can never get back. I decided not to live that way anymore. I didn't do it on my own. God gives us the strength to slow down. Slowing down gives us hope.

1 Corinthians 11:33 Wherefore, my brethren, when ye come together to eat, tarry one for another.

Life does not have to cost so much. I got back in from my walk and I was thinking I needed to buy

something, but actually we already had it – or something that will feasibly work, for the job I need to do. I have made a resolution to buy only functional things that are necessary. I sold things that we no longer used. I now have found out that generic products are adequate and buying used items can also be a solution. Buying in bulk saves money and we can share with a friend. We sold our expensive home and built an affordable one. We sold our expensive vehicles and bought used. We have paid off and cut up our credit cards. We have basic services instead of premium services. We walk, bicycle or carpool when we can. Each month, we work toward cutting expenses and eventually being debt-free. God tells us that a borrower is a slave to a lender. I'm paying off my debts. Over time, we have seen progress and

Proverbs 22:7 The rich ruleth over the poor, and the borrower is servant to the lender.

it encourages us. God is helping us make good choices every day. Less burden of debt gives us hope.

Life does not have to be stressful. I'm going to go to bed now. I can relax and actually sleep, because I learned that everything does not have to cause anxiety. I was on medications for depression and anxiety, but these solutions come with multiple side-effects. I think we need to itemize the things that cause us stress and eliminate them, instead of tolerating them. Nothing is worth the stress. Our perspective needs to be healthy, so that little things aren't causing us big ulcers. If God is for us, who can be against us? We are not in control - God is. He says to be still and know that He is God.

I reflect on that before I go to sleep. I have learned that if the job causes stress, I can pray for a new one and take action to replace the job. If friends cause stress, I can see less of them. If commitments cause stress, I can say "no." If I get out of the way, and let God exert His will in my life, I have the perfect answer every time. I thank God that we can give Him all our stress. Less stress gives us hope.

2 Thessalonians 2:2 That ye be not soon shaken in mind, or be troubled, neither by spirit, nor by word, nor by letter as from us, as that the day of Christ is at hand.

Thank you, God, for the many opportunities to simplify!

Grandma's Cures

Cure #1 CLEAN YOUR JEWELRY

You can clean your gold and silver jewelry with a 2:1 water to ammonia mixture, respectively. After soaking, use a toothbrush to clean all surfaces. Simply let dry, then wipe with a clean cloth. This is not for pearls or jewelry with glue or other types of fragile jewelry.

Cure #2 REMOVE MUSTARD STAINS

You can get mustard stains out of clothing! Before you wash the clothing, make a paste with powdered dishwasher soap and water. Rub the moistened paste onto the stain and let it sit. Then, wash as usual! If stain is still present, do not dry the clothing; reapply paste.

Cure #3 CLEAN WINDOWS

Put 2 tablespoons of white vinegar in a large spray bottle of water, and apply to your windows. Wipe windows clean with newspaper. Reapply for stubborn stains. Windows will be streak-free when dried with newspaper!

forest paths unknown

The forest path is both deeply dark with shadows and brightly lit with sun.

The *destination*... is that the walk will be complete. It isn't the *finish* that we strive for: that is inevitable.

The journey is the prized possession; the discovery along the way - the memories that we treasure. Celebrate and absorb each moment, as it forever becomes a part of you...

We can sail on a big ocean
or we can sail on a small lake.
Don't fret about destination:
its about the journey we make.

We can follow the changing wind,
or try to wear the captain's hat.
I like to let God steer the boat,
while I bow down to have a chat.

No matter, if you're the captain,
or if you be one of the crew.
You might not realize it now,
but God is watching over you!

Sharing Life's Journey

2 Corinthians 4:6 For God,
who commanded the light to shine
out of darkness, hath shined in our hearts,
to give the light of the knowledge
of the glory of God
in the face of Jesus Christ.

1 Corinthians 6:20 For ye are bought with
a price: therefore glorify God in your body,
and in your spirit, which are God's.

Read the Bible and study the Word of God.
God gives us hope!

2 Thessalonians 2:16 Now our Lord Jesus Christ himself, and God, even our Father, which hath loved us, and hath given us everlasting consolation and good hope through grace, 2 Thessalonians 2:17 Comfort your hearts, and stablish you in every good word and work.

Compassion

I clutched her hand, with those beautifully polished nails, resting on the arm of her wheelchair; her eager eyes and expectant smile waited to greet me - always positioned in the same spot in the hallway. Helen, with the beautiful snow white hair and endearing charm was one of the many residents at the nursing home that I'd come to know and love, even though it was my dad I went to visit daily. I felt privileged to learn about the lives of former soldiers, business managers, farmers, waitresses and lawyers; of the residents' interests that they were willing to share with a stranger. A listening ear opens that realm of friendship, which is a precious commodity with unlimited rewards.

God has a way of finding a person where they are in life and bringing ordinary circumstances into a purposeful light. The year my dad spent as a resident in the nursing home gave him, and me, a different kind of time together - a new perspective on what we needed from each other - and a focus on where He wanted us to be looking and what He wanted us to be learning. My dad had questionable faith, and in that year I would read devotionals and he would listen. I honestly don't know how much he absorbed and took to heart, but I felt that tug of the Holy Spirit telling me to continue and pray about it. It was a lesson for both of us. Learning patience in slowing the pace as we took wheelchair strolls inside and outside the facility, learning to see love in so many people's faces, even among the ones who were hurting or ready to give up. We were learning to laugh, when

2 Corinthians 3:18
But we all,
with open face
beholding as in a glass
the glory of the Lord,
are changed
into the same image
from
glory to glory,
even as by the Spirit
of the Lord.

many situations really didn't seem humorous, but the Lord has a way of lightening a moment when we ask Him for help.

A person has to open their eyes and look through God's vision to truly feel His presence. I could walk into the care facility and see so much…everything from pain to loneliness, to despondency, but if I held that dim outlook of every-thing and of everyone, it would be an earthly view. In listening to God and seeing His plan for all who believe, I could see compassion, hope, and trust evident in caregivers, staff and the residents themselves.

I won't forget residents like Helen, who shared her memories of her family, her faith and wonderful years being in a fine arts club - and John, who served proudly for many years in the army, his Bible and his lovely wife, Joyce, by his bedside daily. We all struggle; we all manage to survive in our earthly existence, but we realize the real treasure is waiting for us, at our final rest stop, promising eternal joy with our Savior.

Matthew 6:21 For where
your treasure is,
there will your heart be also.

John 4:36 And he that reapeth
receiveth wages,
and gathereth fruit unto life eternal:
that both he that soweth
and he that reapeth
may rejoice together.

sweet
fresh
berries

Strawberry Preserves

Gather enough cleaned strawberries to yield 4 cups of mashed berries. Put these in a saucepan with 4 cups of sugar and 1/4 of a cup of lemon juice. Over low heat, stir continually until the sugar dissolves completely. Gradually increase the heat until the mixture boils and reaches 225 degrees F.

Pour mixture into hot canning jars that are sterile. Leave space of about 1/2 of an inch at the top and seal with the lids. Process in a normal water bath, according to safe canning practices.

Makes about 5 cups or five of the small 8-ounce jelly jars.

Deep Dish Blueberry Pie

You will need 1 pie shell.

Mix 4 cups of fresh blueberries, 3/4 of a cup of sugar, 1-1/2 tablespooons of tapioca, 1/8 teaspoon of salt, and 1 teaspoon of lemon juice.

Put the mixture in an oblong 10"x6"x2" baking dish. Dot 1 tablespoon of butter over the berries. Roll dough to a rectangular shape, 1/8 of an inch thick. Fit dough over berries. Make a crimped edge. Cut slits for steam to escape.

Bake at 425 degrees F for 40 to 45 minutes. Makes 1 pie.

sweet
fresh
berries

Luke 8:15 But that on
the good ground are they,
which in an honest and good heart,
having heard the word, keep it,
and bring forth fruit
with patience.

Bean and Ham Soup

Make a glaze with 3/4 of a cup of brown sugar and a tablespoon of mustard and 3 tablespoons of water. Spread it onto a small ham and bake in an oven-safe casserole dish with 2 cups of water for an hour at 325 degrees F. In a small pan with butter, cook 1/2 of a cup of baby carrots and one half of a cup of peas, until tender.

Cut baked ham into 1/2" squares and put into an oven-safe casserole dish. Pour in all juices from baking the ham. Add 2 cans of great northern beans, 1 can butter beans and 1 can of pinto beans (use all liquid from the beans.) Add seasoned salt, minced onion and coarse ground pepper to taste. Add carrots and peas. Add 4 cups of water.

Bake at 300 degrees F for 3 hours. Makes 4 generous servings.

John 15:4 Abide in me,
and I in you.
As the branch cannot bear fruit of itself,
except it abide in the vine;
no more can ye,
except ye abide in me.

James 3:17 But the wisdom
that is from above is first pure,
then peaceable, gentle,
and easy to be entreated, full of mercy
and good fruits, without partiality,
and without hypocrisy.

Kuchen (German Pastry)

Crust: 1 cup of sugar, 3 heaping tablespoons of butter-flavored Crisco, or shortening, 2 cups of milk, 5 teaspoons of baking powder, 5 cups of flour - or more - if dough is too soft. Press in pie tins with fingers, spread filling on top. (I double the filling recipe!)

Filling: 2 eggs, 1/2 cup of sugar (I mix a little brown sugar with the white), 2 cups of cream and 1 teaspoon of vanilla. Cook until slightly thickened. Sprinkle sugar and cinnamon on top of the filing. (Can crush graham crackers to add to the sugar and sprinkle on top.)

Bake at 350 degrees F until crust is light brown. Makes 2 pies.

Cooking, canning and baking...

share your favorites with family, friends, co-workers and neighbors!

Jeremiah 17:7
Blessed is the man
that trusteth in the LORD,
and whose hope
the LORD is.

love

1 Corinthians 13:13
And now abideth faith, hope, charity, these three;
but the greatest of these is charity.

Matthew 25:35 For I was an hungered, and ye gave me meat: I was thirsty, and ye gave me drink: I was a stranger, and ye took me in:

Matthew 25:36 Naked, and ye clothed me: I was sick, and ye visited me: I was in prison, and ye came unto me.

Matthew 25:37 Then shall the righteous answer him, saying, Lord, when saw we thee an hungered, and fed thee? or thirsty, and gave thee drink?

Matthew 25:38 When saw we thee a stranger, and took thee in? or naked, and clothed thee?

Matthew 25:39 Or when saw we thee sick, or in prison, and came unto thee?

Matthew 25:40 And the King shall answer and say unto them, Verily I say unto you, Inasmuch as ye have done it unto one of the least of these my brethren, ye have done it unto me.

James 1:27 Pure religion and undefiled before God and the Father is this, To visit the fatherless and widows in their affliction, and to keep himself unspotted from the world.

James 1:22 But be ye doers of the word, and not hearers only, deceiving your own selves.

Choosing to Love and Honor

Something beautiful catches your eye. You love it; you desire to have it. A special someone captures your heart and you proclaim your love for them. A certain food shown in a magazine looks tantalizing and inviting and you'd love to taste it. We acquire tastes and preferences for objects, food and people - and the word 'love' is associated with a strong attachment or feeling belonging to the object or person we treasure or admire.

The casual use of the term 'love' undermines the significance of what God has intended it for in our daily lives. He wants us to first seek HIS love, which enables the Holy Spirit to produce in us God-granted gifts, or fruits of the Spirit.

Galatians 5:22 But the fruit of the Spirit is love, joy, peace, longsuffering, gentleness, goodness, faith, Galatians 5:23 Meekness, temperance: against such there is no law.

Proverbs 9:10 The fear of the LORD is the beginning of wisdom: and the knowledge of the holy is understanding.
Proverbs 9:11 For by me thy days shall be multiplied, and the years of thy life shall be increased.

Job 12:12 With the ancient is wisdom; and in length of days understanding.

2 Timothy 1:7 For God hath not given us the spirit of fear; but of power, and of love, and of a sound mind.

When you consider all these qualities, that feeling of love naturally allows a culmination of these traits to occur. When you have a commitment to the Lord in

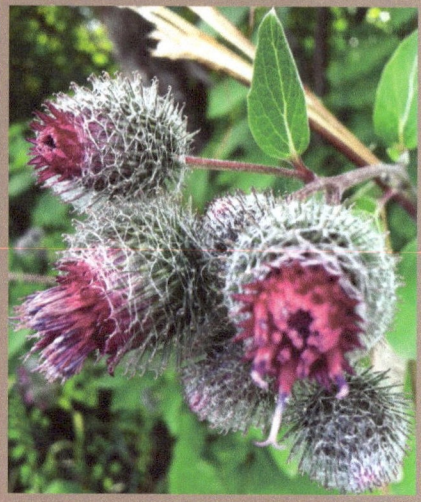

accepting His love, He is also the one who carries us through the turbulence. He carries us through, when those feelings we have for others don't come so 'naturally', whether related to a long relationship or marriage that has waned - or when we have conflicts within personalities and the day-to-day mundaneness becomes an obligation, rather than an easy, 'loving' response.

Feelings themselves are all well and good, but as with choosing to follow the Lord and his guidance, we also 'choose' to love others in our lives, especially in a marriage; committing to caring and praying for direction.

1 John 4:16 And we have known and believed the love that God hath to us. God is love; and he that dwelleth in love dwelleth in God, and God in him.
1 John 4:17 Herein is our love made perfect, that we may have boldness in the day of judgment: because as he is, so are we in this world.
1 John 4:18 There is no fear in love; but perfect love casteth out fear: because fear hath torment. He that feareth is not made perfect in love.

Jude 1:2 Mercy unto you, and peace, and love, be multiplied.

blossom fragrances

Snow gives way to torrential rains and inconvenient mud fills our spring days, depressing our minds for what seems like an endless period of time. Then, suddenly, one day flower and tree buds emerge! Tiny bits of color burst into a brown and gray landscape. Tender, new life that gives us hope and refreshes our spirits! Almost overnight, there are blossoming flowers and flourishing trees everywhere! Seemingly energized, we are compelled to celebrate this life, and drink in the sweet fragrances!

Colors anticipated, we absorb the sweet smells that refresh our spirits. We carefully choose one bloom to carry with us; that we will put in a vase to savor each day. Walking in the neighborhood we see the flowers each person has nurtured. We admire and share all we have, for we know it is only for a short time.

Psalm 103:12 As far as the east is from the west, so far hath he removed our transgressions from us.

WHAT CAN WE DO OR MAKE, TOGETHER?

Preserve Strawberries

Embroidery

Woodworking

Can Vegetables

Sew

DIY Projects

Make Candles

Drink Hot Cider

Collect Rocks

Dry Flowers

Restore Antiques

Quilting

Make Chicken Soup

Grow a Garden

Study the Bible

Teaching Old-fashioned Traditions

The winding way home is very long. It gives a person time to think.

Well off the beaten path, our cabin takes a while to get to, once you leave the main road. We have to drive under the interstate highway, through a tunnel that is covered in graffiti. The curvy public road ends and the private road begins. The wooded and secluded setting is an ideal place to escape from the world. We have one sweet neighbor family nearby. As we drive on in to our property we see deer, rabbits, turkeys, birds, snakes and occasionally we spot a wildcat. The sunsets we see from the long private road are incredible - with vivid pinks, searing oranges, deep purples and intense blues!

We break down over the hill, bouncing down our rocky driveway and it is a series of twists and turns; ups and downs. Most people close their eyes when they first ride in with us to visit. The last part of the driveway is straight up – and the cabin sits in the middle of the forest. It is heavenly.

When we walk into our simple little cabin, we shut the door with a *whoosh*! Suddenly, we are in a place that is separate from the world. With enough food stored, we wouldn't have to leave for a month!

Many people would be bored, being isolated, but I was blessed with a childhood rich in adventure, education, great imagination and varied experiences. My mom, dad and grandmother were great teachers.

My mom enriched life with puzzles, French language, piano, cooking, crafts and game-playing, as well as a plethora of other things! Mom read me numerous books for hours. I felt like I had traveled the world! I wanted to be a writer. When I was little, I had imaginary friends! Mom and I read about wild plants that were edible and made candied

violets. We laughed like fools and did silly things. We have many traditions and they are precious. We sewed clothing; even my prom dress. We had food fights and played pranks. We played Chinese Checkers and Canasta and she didn't let me win. I had to earn it. My pouting didn't help the odds at all – and I kept coming back for more! We have wonderful, long talks. We spent hours identifying the flowers, trees and insects. We picked blackberries and enjoyed hours in the creek. Tromping through the snowy woods as a family, we chose the Christmas tree, sawed it down and hauled it home. Mom and I made many ornate, intricate ornaments! I oil painted and drew and started so many projects. She said I started way too many things and never finished them. That was a good observation - and is still true, today! With God's help, I am able to finish projects that glorify Him! I think projects in various stages of completion are a security blanket.

Some people don't have any projects, but I think they are an important key to enjoying life. I can't imagine being bored! Life is rich, because people invested in me, when I was young. My skills are enjoyable, a ministry, allow me to identify with others and help me to earn a living.

Proverbs 22:6 Train up a child in the way he should go: and when he is old, he will not depart from it.

When I was young, we would arrive at grandma's house and hurry inside, shutting the door with a *whoosh*! It was warm; with a smell of the wood stove permeating the house. When I say wood stove, I mean the cast-iron cook stove in the kitchen, complete with four burners and filled with kindling wood that was burning. The cast iron pans were filled: one with soup and one with potatoes, ground beef and onions. It smelled heavenly. Even in her seventies, grandma would walk in the woods, break sticks into smaller pieces on her knees - and carry them home. We used to go for long walks. She

would tell me to rest and sit down on some moss in the shade. We always found the prettiest, greenest moss. Then, she would bring out the cloth handkerchief… a little white one, embroidered with pretty flowers. Inside the handkerchief there were two cookies: one for her and one for me. She taught me to crochet and to make rugs out of plastic bread wrapper bags. She sewed on a 1920s era cast-iron treadle sewing machine and she let me use it. Once, I made a mistake with that cast-iron beauty and the needle went right through my fingernail. Luckily, she didn't see it and I hid the blood - and the pain. She sewed and never wasted even a bit of thread. She reused paper bags over and over - and sewed the ones that had become torn. I wondered about that. How could life be that desperate? She had had 13 children. What a life she lived – with so much appreciation and passion for the birds, her gardens and the playhouse she made for all the grandchildren. Old plates and pans and bowls, she had painted silver! We pretended and made mud pies; "played house" well into the dark! At the end of a long day, we climbed onto the big porch swing and covered up with blankets, felt the fresh night air on our noses and listened to the peepers. All of these were traditions and are now precious memories.

Growing up a tomboy, I spent a lot of time with my dad in the summer. It was fun to do construction work and to mow lawns. We always stopped at little stores along the way, just to rest and enjoy a Hershey's® Bar and an Orange Crush® soda. Dad would pop the metal top off the glass soda bottle, by putting it someplace in the open truck door. Some piece of metal in the door worked perfectly. He also bought us Dixie® Cup ice cream cups with the little wooden spoons. We would sit and slowly eat them. We worked at home, too, in the

Matthew 5:16 Let your light so shine before men, that they may see your good works, and glorify your Father which is in heaven.

garage where I sorted nuts, bolts, screws and tools. I used to soak the gears for transmissions in big tubs of oil and I took a big wire brush to clean all types of truck parts or welds. Dad welded and I watched with a mask, as he produced the metal supports for wooden docks at the nearby lake. I painted them. To heat the house, we cut our own wood and hauled it in - many times late on a school night. Dad has big trucks and in the past, many times, they had mechanical problems. We went across the lake one time on a small ferry, in a huge dump truck that had no brakes! He kept it in gear and we went a little forward or a little backward to stay in place. For some reason, we could not just shut it off, in gear. It had to stay running. I could imagine rolling off the ferry into the deep water of the lake! But, as usual, we were safe. Life was hard, risky, rewarding and worthwhile. We could be proud of everything we did, because we did our best. These were our traditions and they are precious.

We need to share traditions or they will be lost. We need to share the hobbies, stories, art, and music. We can help grandchildren, church youth, seniors, friends, children, neighbors, and community teens reveal their talents, develop coping skills and nurture a *passion for living!*

Not one of these types of activities involves virtual reality or a distracting cell phone, video game console, internet, TV or computer.

God loves everyone and we can show His love by nurturing people - helping them discover their hidden talents and gifts - at any age! Sharing the old-fashioned traditions brings joy and gives hope!

Hebrews 6:10
For God is not unrighteous to forget your work and labour of love, which ye have shown toward his name, in that ye have ministered to the saints, and do minister.

gifts

We were born with special gifts from God. We also have natural talents from God. But, each and every one of us has a supernatural spiritual gift or gifts, given by God. Our gift is like an open door through which we walk hand in hand, like a child, with the Holy Spirit! It is a holy gift: all we have to do is accept it and embrace it! We can touch other people in a way that is spiritual, as God directs. Using our spiritual gifts brings Glory to God!

Ephesians 4:7 But unto every one of us
is given grace according
to the measure of the gift of Christ.

Father, as we read the Bible and pray, let us know what our gifts are. Please, let us do wonderful things for you! Let us reach out and love our neighbors. Let us strengthen them, lift them up and cause them to praise your name!

Our gift is a tool and a calling from the Lord, enabling us to fulfill the great commission!

1 Corinthians 12:28
And God hath set some in the church, first apostles, secondarily prophets, thirdly teachers, after that miracles, then gifts of healings, helps, governments, diversities of tongues.

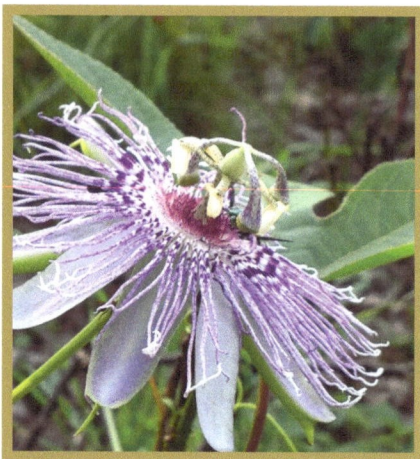

1 Corinthians 12:8-11
For to one is given by the Spirit the word of wisdom; to another the word of knowledge by the same Spirit;
To another faith by the same Spirit; to another the gifts of healing by the same Spirit;
To another the working of miracles; to another prophecy; to another discerning of spirits; to another divers kinds of tongues; to another the interpretation of tongues:
But all these worketh that one and the selfsame Spirit, dividing to every man severally as he will.

Ephesians 4:11 And he gave some, apostles; and some, prophets; and some, evangelists; and some, pastors and teachers;
Ephesians 4:12 For the perfecting of the saints, for the work of the ministry, for the edifying of the body of Christ:
Ephesians 4:13 Till we all come in the unity of the faith, and of the knowledge of the Son of God, unto a perfect man, unto the measure of the stature of the fulness of Christ:
Ephesians 4:14 That we henceforth be no more children, tossed to and fro, and carried about with every wind of doctrine, by the sleight of men, and cunning craftiness, whereby they lie in wait to deceive;
Ephesians 4:15 But speaking the truth in love, may grow up into him in all things, which is the head, even Christ:
Ephesians 4:16 From whom the whole body fitly joined together and compacted by that which every joint supplieth, according to the effectual working in the measure of every part, maketh increase of the body unto the edifying of itself in love.

We have been given spiritual gifts to use in this life. It is a gift of grace. Jesus prayed to God and God sent us the Holy Spirit! Each Christian has a special gift to uplift the body of Christ and to bring Glory to God. We have a responsibility to let the Holy Spirit work through us.

When we use our spiritual gifts, others will see the fruits of the Spirit. Our demeanor will change, and we will be kind to one another, tenderhearted and forgiving. By our actions, we can truly inspire friends, family, co-workers and neighbors. When we consider that the Holy Spirit lives within each of us, we realize that we are never alone!

The Lord is My Rock.

John 14:16
And I will pray the Father, and
he shall give you
another Comforter, that he
may abide with you for ever;
John 14:17
Even the Spirit of truth; whom
the world cannot receive,
because it seeth him not,
neither knoweth him: but ye
know him; for he dwelleth
with you, and shall be in you.

Romans 15:13
Now the God of hope
fill you with all joy and peace
in believing, that ye may
abound in hope, through the
power of the Holy Ghost.

Psalm 18:2
The LORD is my rock, and my
fortress, and my deliverer; my
God, my strength, in whom I
will trust; my buckler,
and the horn of my salvation,
and my high tower.

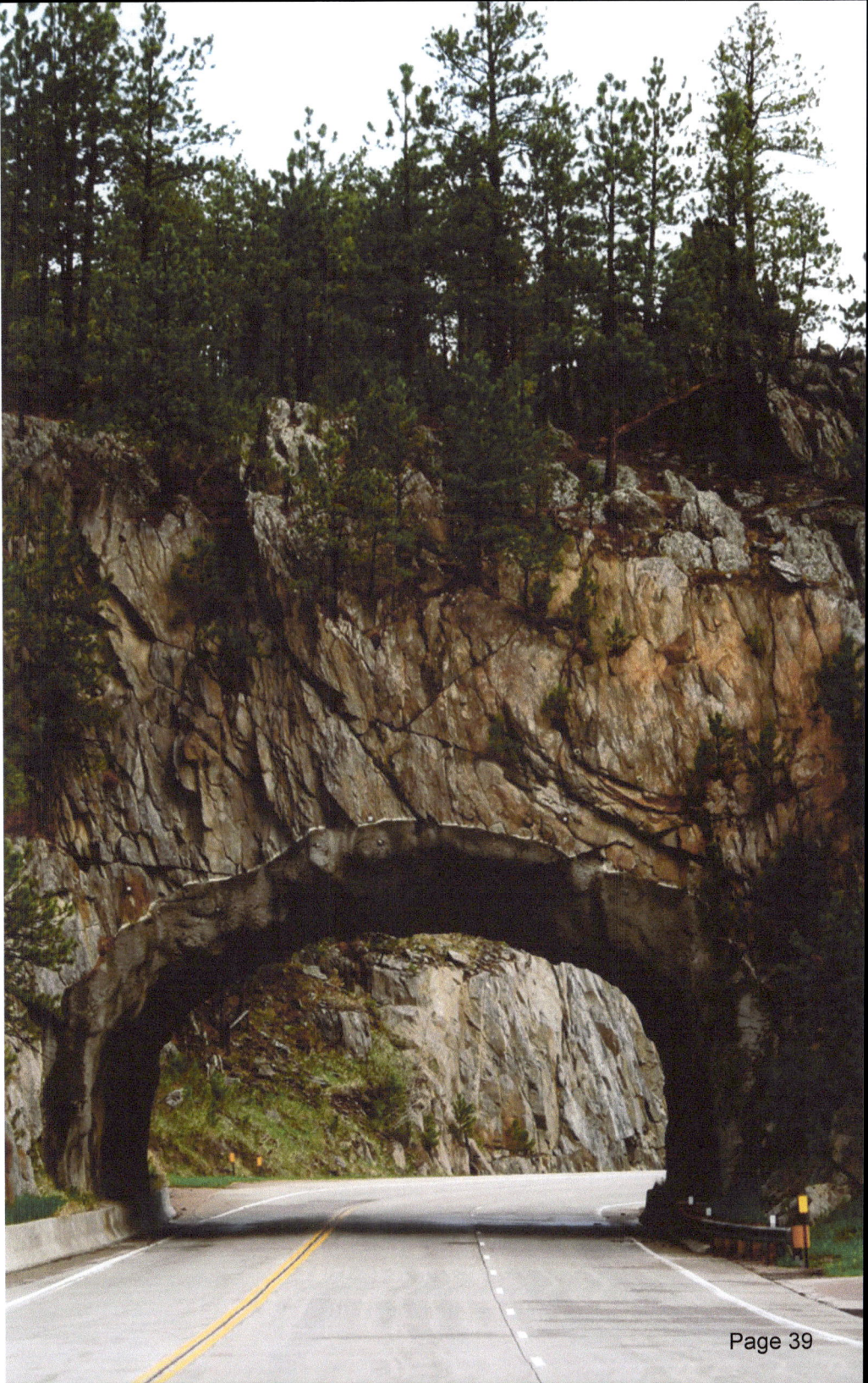

spring

Philippians 4:8
Finally, brethren, whatsoever things are true, whatsoever things are honest, whatsoever things are just, whatsoever things are pure, whatsoever things are lovely, whatsoever things are of good report; if there be any virtue, and if there be any praise, think on these things.

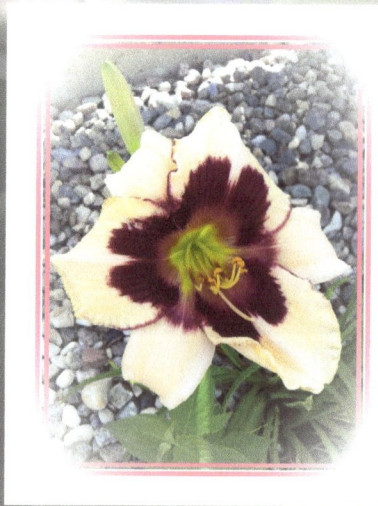

Read the Bible
and study the Word of God.
God gives us hope!

Pathway of Faith

"Great is thy faithfulness, great is thy faithfulness… morning by morning new mercies I see."

We love the old hymn that never fails to give us new hope in its lyrics and the promise given to us through our Savior. By believing in Him and putting our faith in the Lord, He gives us the assurance of salvation and the promise of eternity with Him. With faith, comes obedience, in our thoughts, actions and daily walk, following in the direction He yearns to lead us.

Romans 1:5 By whom we have received grace and apostleship, for obedience to the faith among all nations, for his name: Romans 1:6 Among whom are ye also the called of Jesus Christ:

As we rise each morning, we are called and awakened to have faith in what is set before us. The Lord gives us mercy; He gives us hope as His children, to believe and to live according to what He has set before us. We can choose to ignore or to open our eyes to see every circumstance; every part of our own life plan orchestrated by Him for our good - for His purpose.

"Summer and winter and springtime and harvest. Sun, moon and stars in their courses above join with all nature in manifold witness to thy great faithfulness, mercy and love."

Putting our faith and trust in Jesus allows us to grow, flourish and reach out to others as He guides us on a clearcut path - a directive for life - according to Him.

Psalm 1:3 And he shall be like a tree planted by the rivers of water, that bringeth forth his fruit in his season; his leaf also shall not wither; and whatsoever he doeth shall prosper.

If we are clouded by setbacks or hardships, He still allows a clear vision ahead if we are faithful in the journey with Him. If we thirst for knowledge, His Word provides the answers. If we struggle with others in relationships, He offers the fruit of forgiveness and reconciliation in His teachings. If we cannot let go of troublesome circumstances, His mercy allows us to let go, and let HIM take that burden.

"Pardon for sin and a peace that endureth, thine own dear presence to cheer and to guide. Strength for today and bright hope for tomorrow. Blessings all mine, with ten thousand beside!

As we believe, He blesses greatly!

Proverbs 4:18 But the path of the just is as the shining light, that shineth more and more unto the perfect day.

Trust the Lord always and be faithful in His name and His word.

Malachi 4:2 But unto you that fear my name shall the Sun of righteousness arise with healing in his wings; and ye shall go forth, and grow up as calves of the stall.

Great Is Thy Faithfulness by William M. Runyan

Pathway of Faith

Hebrews 11:1

Now faith is the substance of things hoped for, the evidence of things not seen.

Proverbs 3:5 Trust in the LORD with all thine heart; and lean not unto thine own understanding.
Pr 3:6 In all thy ways acknowledge him, and he shall direct thy paths.

Luke 3:4 As it is written in the book of the words of Esaias the prophet, saying, The voice of one crying in the wilderness, Prepare ye the way of the Lord, make his paths straight.

Father

Father in Heaven, you are the hope we reach for!
You give the breath of life each precious day.
You provide all our needs: we only have to pray!
We thank you for many blessings, rich or poor.

You show us your mercy and you show us your love.
Thank you for your holy grace and Jesus, your Son.
He paid the debt for all our sins: every one.
Father, we know that you're watching from above!

We want to be good children; know our role we play.
Father, help us to display mercy as from above.
Father, please help us live with the spirit of love.
Let us shine your light in the dark - showing the way!

By the Holy Spirit's power, in Jesus' name pray.
For the Glory of God above... we only ask...
Truly, we seek wisdom and strength to do the task.
How hard can it be, to love our neighbors each day?

Father, sometimes we wander thru life hand-in-hand.
Other times we feel lost and hopeless; all alone.
Then, we realize your love when we are full grown.
You carried us: one set of footprints in the sand!

Thank you for loving us, Father in Heaven!

Matthew 18:3 And said, Verily I say unto you, Except ye be converted, and become as little children, ye shall not enter into the kingdom of heaven.

Wandering through Life

We are never alone.

Isaiah 6:3 And one cried unto another, and said, Holy, holy, holy, is the LORD of hosts: the whole earth is full of his glory.

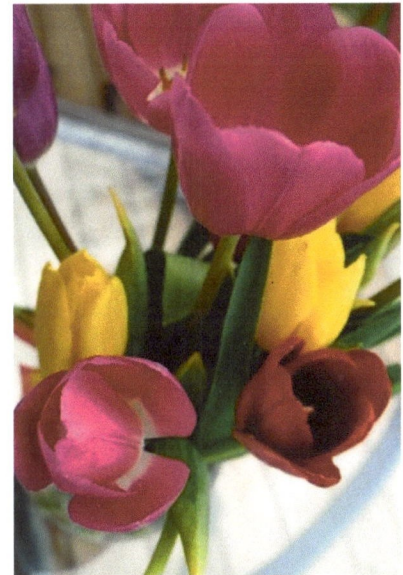

Psalm 17:15 As for me, I will behold thy face in righteousness: I shall be satisfied, when I awake, with thy likeness.

Psalm 33:22 Let thy mercy, O LORD, be upon us, according as we hope in thee.

Wandering through Life

We are never alone.

1 John 4:4 Ye are of God, little children, and have overcome them: because greater is he that is in you, than he that is in the world.

John 3:16 For God so loved the world, that he gave his only begotten Son, that whosoever believeth in him should not perish, but have everlasting life.

John 3:17 For God sent not his Son into the world to condemn the world; but that the world through him might be saved.

Read the Bible and study the Word of God. God gives us hope!

HopeforNeighbors.com

sunrise

Romans 5:1 Therefore being justified by faith, we have peace with God through our Lord Jesus Christ:
Romans 5:2 By whom also we have access by faith into this grace wherein we stand, and rejoice in hope of the glory of God.
Romans 5:3 And not only so, but we glory in tribulations also: knowing that tribulation worketh patience;
Romans 5:4 And patience, experience; and experience, hope:
Romans 5:5 And hope maketh not ashamed; because the love of God is shed abroad in our hearts by the Holy Ghost which is given unto us.

Read the Bible and study the Word of God. God gives us hope!

Romans 8:31 What
shall we then say
to these things?
If God be for us,
who can be against us?

Hope for Neighbors™

Matthew 22:37 Jesus said unto him, Thou shalt love the Lord
thy God with all thy heart, and with all thy soul, and with all thy mind.
Matthew 22:38 This is the first and great commandment.
Matthew 22:39 And the second is like unto it,
Thou shalt love thy neighbour as thyself.

www.HopeforNeighbors.com

www.ingramcontent.com/pod-product-compliance
Lightning Source LLC
Chambersburg PA
CBHW042010090426

42811CB00015B/1605